First Picture Dictionary
Animals
第一本图画词典
动物

Pig
猪

Rabbit
兔子

Butterfly
蝴蝶

Fox
狐狸

Illustrated by Anna Ivanir

www.kidkiddos.com
Copyright ©2025 by KidKiddos Books Ltd.
support@kidkiddos.com

All rights reserved. No part of this book may be reproduced in any form or by any electronic or mechanical means, including information storage and retrieval systems, without written permission from the publisher, except in the case of a reviewer, who may quote brief passages embodied in critical articles or in a review.
First edition, 2025

Library and Archives Canada Cataloguing in Publication
First Picture Dictionary - Animals (English Simplified Chinese Bilingual edition)
ISBN: 978-1-83416-411-3 paperback
ISBN: 978-1-83416-412-0 hardcover
ISBN: 978-1-83416-410-6 eBook

Wild Animals
野生动物

Lion
狮子

Tiger
老虎

Giraffe
长颈鹿

✦ *A giraffe is the tallest animal on land.*
✦ 长颈鹿是陆地上最高的动物。

Elephant
大象

Monkey
猴子

Wild Animals
野生动物

Hippopotamus
河马

Panda
熊猫

Fox
狐狸

Rhino
犀牛

Deer
鹿

Moose
驼鹿

Wolf
狼

Squirrel
松鼠

✦*A moose is a great swimmer and can dive underwater to eat plants!*

◆驼鹿是优秀的游泳者，还能潜入水中吃植物！

Koala
树袋熊

✦*A squirrel hides nuts for winter, but sometimes forgets where it put them!*

◆松鼠会把坚果藏起来过冬，但有时会忘记藏在哪儿了！

Gorilla
大猩猩

Pets
宠物

Canary
金丝雀

✦ *A frog can breathe through its skin as well as its lungs!*
✦ 青蛙不仅用肺呼吸，还能通过皮肤呼吸！

Guinea Pig
豚鼠

Frog
青蛙

Hamster
仓鼠

Goldfish
金鱼

Dog
狗

◆ *Some parrots can copy words and even laugh like a human!*
◆ 有些鹦鹉会模仿说话，甚至像人一样笑！

Cat
猫

Parrot
鹦鹉

Animals at the Farm
农场里的动物

Cow
牛

Chicken
鸡

Duck
鸭子

Sheep
绵羊

Horse
马

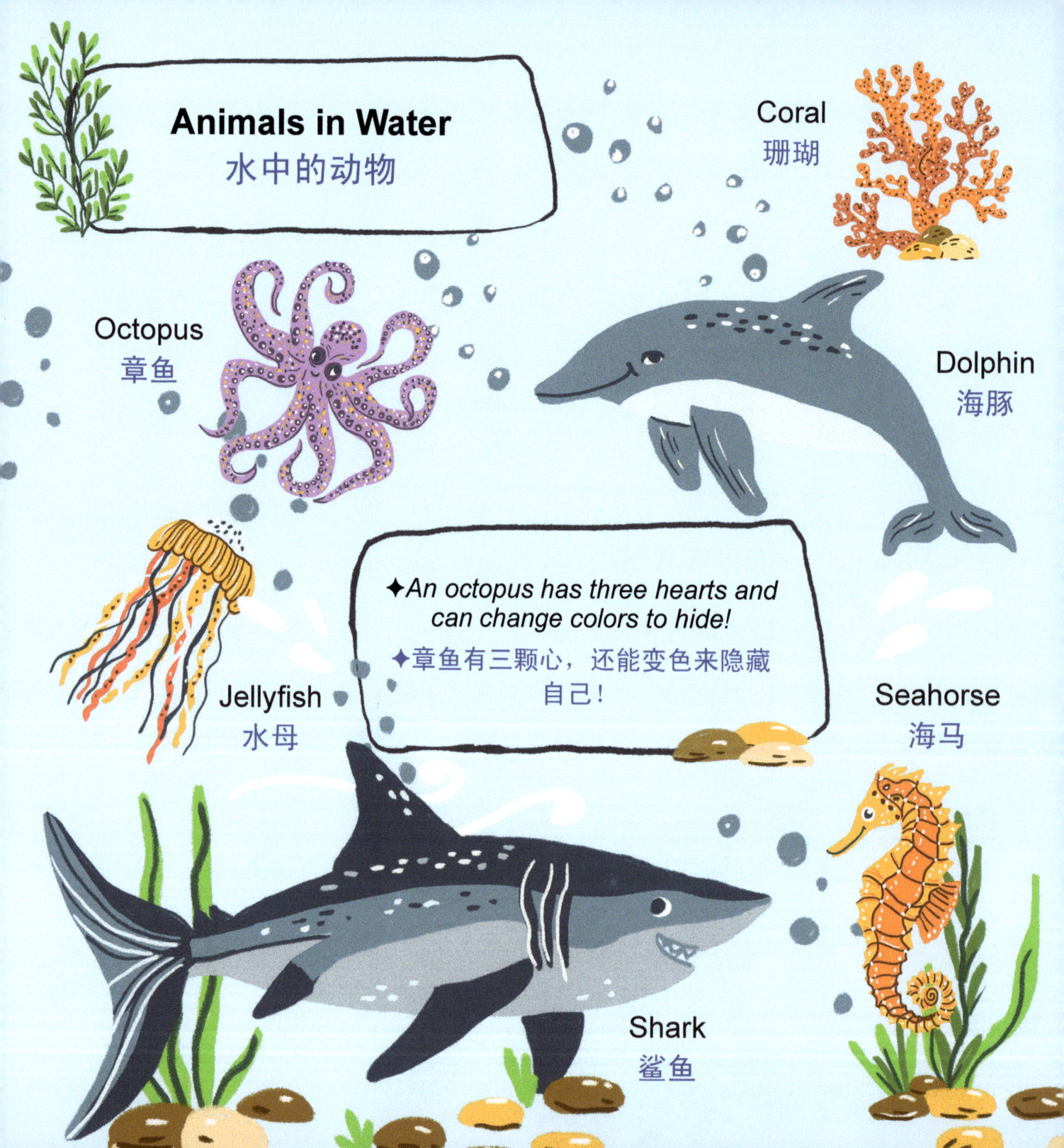

Mosquito
蚊子

Dragonfly
蜻蜓

> ✦*A dragonfly was one of the first insects on Earth, even before dinosaurs!*
> ✦蜻蜓是地球上最早出现的昆虫之一，比恐龙还早！

Butterfly
蝴蝶

Bee
蜜蜂

Ladybug
瓢虫

Wild Cats
野生猫科动物

Puma 美洲狮

Lion 狮子

Cheetah 猎豹

Lynx 猞猁

✦ *A cheetah is the fastest animal on land.*
✦ 猎豹是陆地上跑得最快的动物。

Panther 黑豹

Small Animals
小型动物

Chameleon
变色龙

Spider
蜘蛛

✦ *An ostrich is the biggest bird, but it cannot fly!*
✦ 鸵鸟是最大的鸟类，但它却不会飞！

Bee
蜜蜂

✦ *A snail carries its home on its back and moves very slowly.*
✦ 蜗牛把它的家驮在自己背上，移动的非常缓慢。

Snail
蜗牛

Mouse
老鼠

Quiet Animals
安静的动物

Ladybug
瓢虫

Turtle
乌龟

✦ *A turtle can live both on land and in water.*
✦ 乌龟既能在陆地上生活，也能在水中生活。

Fish
鱼

Lizard
蜥蜴

Owl
猫头鹰

Bat
蝙蝠

✦An owl hunts at night and uses its hearing to find food!
✦猫头鹰在夜间捕猎，用听觉来寻找食物！

✦A firefly glows at night to find other fireflies.
✦萤火虫在夜间发光，是为了找到其他萤火虫。

Raccoon
浣熊

Tarantula
食鸟蛛

Colorful Animals
色彩缤纷的动物们

A flamingo is pink
火烈鸟是粉红色的

An owl is brown
猫头鹰是棕色的

A swan is white
天鹅是白色的

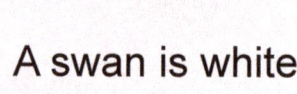

An octopus is purple
章鱼是紫色的

A frog is green
青蛙是绿色的

✦ *A frog is green, so it can hide among the leaves.*

✦ 青蛙是绿色的，所以它可以藏在树叶中。

Animals and Their Babies
动物和它们的宝宝

Cow and Calf
母牛和小牛

Cat and Kitten
猫和小猫

Chicken and Chick
母鸡和小鸡

✦ *A chick talks to its mother even before it hatches.*
✦ 小鸡在孵化前就能和妈妈"说话"。

Dog and Puppy
狗和小狗

Butterfly and Caterpillar
蝴蝶和毛毛虫

Sheep and Lamb
绵羊和小羊

Horse and Foal
马和小马

Pig and Piglet
猪和小猪

Goat and Kid
山羊和小羊

www.ingramcontent.com/pod-product-compliance
Lightning Source LLC
LaVergne TN
LVHW072002060526
838200LV00010B/257

Animals and Their Babies
Animaux et leurs petits

Cow and Calf
Vache et Veau

Cat and Kitten
Chat et Chaton

✦ A chick talks to its mother even before it hatches.
✦ *Un poussin parle à sa mère même avant d'éclore.*

Chicken and Chick
Poule et Poussin

Dog and Puppy
Chien et Chiot

Butterfly and Caterpillar
Papillon et Chenille

Sheep and Lamb
Mouton et Agneau

Horse and Foal
Cheval et Poulain

Pig and Piglet
Cochon et Porcelet

Goat and Kid
Chèvre et Chevreau

www.ingramcontent.com/pod-product-compliance
Lightning Source LLC
LaVergne TN
LVHW072002060526
838200LV00010B/260